Original title:
Life: The Ultimate Riddle

Copyright © 2025 Creative Arts Management OÜ
All rights reserved.

Author: Julian Montgomery
ISBN HARDBACK: 978-1-80566-248-8
ISBN PAPERBACK: 978-1-80566-543-4

Serendipity's Secrets

In a world where ducks wear hats,
Chasing rainbows on little chats.
Sunshine giggles between the trees,
Ice cream cones dance in summer breeze.

Mismatched socks lead to golden rocks,
Finding treasure where time unlocks.
Wombats in slippers make quite the scene,
Whispering secrets of what might have been.

The Symphony of Experiences

Life plays on, a wacky tune,
Under the glow of a laughing moon.
Pants that squeak with every stride,
Turtles racing in a waterslide.

Cupcakes sing in flavors bold,
While wishes burst like stories told.
Juggling dreams, they stumble and fall,
Yet laughter echoes; it conquers all.

The Riddle of Existence

Balancing eggs on a spoon so tight,
While cats wear ties and dance at night.
Jigsaw pieces in colors so bright,
Twists and turns lead to pure delight.

Finding answers in quirky places,
Smiles hidden behind silly faces.
The clock sings songs of whimsical time,
As we all dance to the cosmic rhyme.

Chasing Fleeting Thoughts

Socks on a journey to nowhere fast,
Tickling toes as shadows dance past.
A giggle here, a snort right there,
Thoughts take flight, light as the air.

Dreams like bubbles float in the breeze,
Pop! They vanish with laughter's ease.
In pursuit of silliness, we find our way,
Chasing the joy of a brand-new day.

Down the Rabbit Hole

In a world of hats and shoes,
Chasing rabbits, what's the use?
Questions swirl like dizzy bees,
Follow me, if you please!

Tea with time and tales so tall,
Madness echoes through it all.
Tumbling down, what did I find?
Wonders out of the mind!

Circles of Curiosity

A circle drawn with crayons bright,
Why do clouds dance in the night?
Round and round, the questions flow,
Where's the end? Oh, who would know?

Jumps and skips, we laugh and spin,
Clocks are lost, where to begin?
Follow that cat, oh so sly,
What's a riddle without a why?

The Maze of Moments

In a maze where echoes laugh,
I took a turn, or was it half?
Lost my thoughts in a right old twist,
Did I give up, or did I persist?

Ticking clocks with absurd beats,
Chasing cheese or tasty treats?
Do I turn left, or is it right?
Round and round through day and night!

The Gift of Pondering

With a bow and a grin so wide,
Unwrapped thoughts seem to collide.
Why do socks always go astray?
Can't they just choose to stay?

Gifts of questions, all aglow,
What's the meaning? Who would know?
Ponder on, my friend, don't fret,
In the end, we're the best duet!

The Art of Questioning

Why did the chicken cross the lane?
To find the punchline and forget the pain!
Is the grass greener? So I ponder,
Or just a trick of my own wonder?

Why do we giggle at wise old men?
Their answers are puzzles, again and again!
In every riddle hides a clue,
That makes me scratch my head and chew.

The Dance of Causes

If I trip on air, do I float or fall?
Or is it fate just having a ball?
A butterfly flaps, and yet here I sit,
Chasing my tail, oh what a wit!

The jokes of the universe swirl around,
Where cause and effect can easily confound.
Did I choose my path, or was it a jest?
A cosmic riff that leaves me impressed.

The Paradox of Being

I wake up each day, just to complain,
Am I the driver or stuck on a train?
To laugh at my woes is the best defense,
As I stumble through life, it all makes sense!

A puzzle wrapped in a riddle's embrace,
Trying to put on my best happy face.
Is the answer hidden in the next cup?
Or just in the snacks that I can't get enough?

Strings of Fate

I tangled my shoelaces and fell on my face,
Was it fate or a moment lacking grace?
Each choice I make spins a thread so fine,
In the fabric of chaos, I'm dancing divine!

The universe chuckles, what a grand show,
As I waltz to the tune of 'Do I even know?'
With laughter as currency, we barter and play,
In this wild tapestry, we find our way.

Chasing Fleeting Moments

Time flies like a bird that forgot to wear pants,
We laugh at its silliness, join in the dance.
Chasing shadows, we stumble and trip,
Hands in our pockets, ready to skip.

Each second we catch, like bubbles in air,
Pops with a giggle, life's quirky affair.
We chase after laughter, that slippery friend,
Mapping our folly, no need to pretend.

The Chronicles of Wondering Souls

Once was a man with a pensive chin,
Wondered if puzzles were meant to be win.
He pondered the colors of socks in a drawer,
Wondering if answers were hidden in lore.

His cat gave a wink, as if in league,
With the deepest of mysteries, quite a fatigue.
Together they journeyed, no GPS guide,
Just belly laughs, while destiny hides.

The Heart's Unwritten Code

My heart keeps a journal, though no one can read,
It scribbles in riddles, planting the seed.
A dance-off with Cupid, awkward yet sweet,
Tripping on feelings, oh, isn't life neat?

It writes about pizza, the joy of good cheese,
And how socks disappear, like whispers in breeze.
Each crush is a chapter, with twists and with turns,
Leaving me puzzled, while passion still burns.

Labyrinthine Paths of Understanding

In a maze made of thoughts, I search for a clue,
With no map to follow, my mind's in a stew.
I bump into walls, dressed in mismatched socks,
Laughing at wonders, infinite paradox.

Each turn leads to questions, a circle of glee,
If wisdom was chocolate, I'd sweeten my tea.
The paths twist and twirl, like spaghetti on days,
Yet joy in confusion always pays.

Secrets Beneath the Surface

Underneath our sunny smiles,
A jumble of socks waits in piles.
Lost keys dance by the coffee cup,
Who knew chaos could fill us up?

The cat plots while we sip our tea,
With dreams of world domination, you see.
But we're all just here, trying our best,
To find the humor in this quirky quest.

A Journey to the Unknown

Pack your bags; we're off to roam,
To places we won't call home.
With maps upside down, we take our flight,
Who needs GPS when you're just polite?

The food's too spicy, the drinks too sweet,
We stumble along, two left feet.
Yet laughter rings loud, it's clear to see,
The greatest treasure is just being free.

Reflections in Time

Mirrors show us who we've grown,
With every wrinkle, wisdom's shown.
We laugh at styles from days long past,
Was that really a trend? Good grief, what a blast!

Each birthday cake adds more candles here,
Yet we blow them out without any fear.
For time is a jest, a playful parade,
And we all just laugh as the years fade.

The Question of Being

Why do we ponder? Why do we muse?
Is it breakfast cereal or the evening news?
The cosmic joke's in every small thing,
Like socks that go missing, oh what a fling!

Do we dance with shadows or run from the light?
With questions so baffling, we giggle with fright.
Yet here we stand, confusion our friend,
In this riddle of wits, will it ever end?

Mysteries in Motion

Like a squirrel on a quest,
Chasing dreams in a jest,
Finding acorns in the street,
With a waddle and a beat.

Why do socks always hide?
Life's a game, a silly ride,
With laughter and a cheer,
What's behind that door, oh dear?

Mapping out the stars at night,
Who knows what gives them flight?
Are they just a sparkling tease,
Hidden truths in the breeze?

A cat that thinks it's a dog,
Jumping high and in a fog,
Chasing shadows, lost in play,
Wondering what's here to stay.

The Canvas of Questions

Dancing pencils on the page,
Painting quirks in every age,
Why does the chicken cross? Oh, me!
To survey its domain, we agree.

Pies that float on clouds of cream,
What are dreams, or so they seem?
Is it logic wearing a dress,
Or the chaos we confess?

Each wrinkle holds a secret plot,
An enigma while it's hot,
Why do ducks wear silly hats?
To attend parties with friendly cats?

Beneath the stars, a riddle plays,
As they twinkle in a maze,
Is it random, is it fate?
Or a cosmic joke we create?

Beyond the Veil of Understanding

Questions dance like fireflies,
Whispering truths in playful sighs,
Why do we laugh, why do we cry?
In confusion, we all comply.

The cat that knows the universe,
In its purr, a sweet converse,
Knows the secret to the cheese,
And runs off with agile ease.

Riddles wrapped in morning sun,
Chasing each while on the run,
Why did the bird learn to sing?
To distract from the woes we bring.

So here we stand, a jolly crew,
With wonderments both big and few,
Life's surprises, a grand delight,
In every giggle, day and night.

Tales of the Unpredictable

In a hat, a rabbit jumps,
Over puddles, skips the clumps,
Why does the moon wink at me?
It knows all of my secrets, see.

Frogs in bowties sing a tune,
Dancing brightly 'neath the moon,
What if we all made a pact,
To turn back to joy, in fact?

Clouds that wear a silly grin,
Invite us to the fun within,
Why do storms play hide and seek?
To find joy in the cheeky peek.

A treasure hunt in the mundane,
Finding gems in the fast lane,
Every day's a brand new show,
With laughter, frolic, and a glow.

The Whirlwind of Thoughts

My mind's a circus, filled with cheer,
Thoughts dance around, they disappear.
Round and round, like a spinning top,
When will it end? I really can't stop.

Juggling tasks, a clown on parade,
Mistakes pile up, a grand charade.
I trip and fall, the crowd's in stitches,
Who knew my brain had so many glitches?

Questions fly like popcorn popping,
In my head, the laughter's non-stopping.
Why do socks always lose their mates?
Is there a club? Just for odd traits?

So here I twirl in this merry show,
In a riddle dance, I steal the glow.
With every thought, I giggle and grin,
What might it mean? Let the fun begin!

The Essence of Wonder

Wonders bloom like daisies bright,
In the garden of day and night.
Why do birds sing silly songs?
Nature plays where humor belongs.

Butterflies flutter, tickling my nose,
As I ponder why grass grows.
Do ants ever feel overworked?
Or do they laugh while they lurk?

Riddles rise like bubbles afloat,
Why do we take our dreams as a quote?
If I wear my clothes inside out,
Will the world suddenly shout?

Giggles echo in the vast unknown,
Wonders weave in seeds we've sown.
So let's dance and spin around,
In this charming riddle, joy is found!

The Riddle Wrapped in Time

Time ticks on, a quirky beast,
Feeding riddles, never ceased.
Why does my watch always run late?
It must be playing a funny fate.

A clock with arms raised in delight,
As I scramble to grasp the light.
If minutes can skip like a stone,
Are seconds just waiting for the throne?

What's the secret of a week's delay?
Why does Monday feel far away?
Is Tuesday just playing a game,
In the riddle of time, who's to blame?

So let's giggle at our fate with glee,
In this funny puzzle, wild and free.
Wrapped in laughter, we march and rhyme,
In a whimsical whirl, we embrace time!

Threads of Fate Weaving Together

In a loom of chance we stand,
Knots of fate made by hand.
Every twist, a curious thread,
Laughing at what the wise ones said.

Patterns form, then fall away,
Like socks that vanish mid-play.
Tangled up, we trip and spin,
All those prizes we never win.

With stitches of joy and seams of pain,
We dance in sunshine and in rain.
With every loop, a brand-new start,
Who knew chaos was an art?

So let's not fret, let's not complain,
For every tangle holds its gain.
In threads of fate, we play our part,
A patchwork quilt, a hopeful heart.

The Map of Human Experience

I drew a map of all my dreams,
With dotted lines and tangled seams.
X marks the spot where laughter grows,
And all the secrets no one knows.

There are valleys deep of worries wide,
Mountains of pride with nowhere to hide.
A river flows with rivers of tears,
And twisted paths ignore our fears.

Every corner, a riddle to solve,
With puzzle pieces we must evolve.
A compass spins in hilarious ways,
Pointing us back to our silly days.

So let's embrace the crazy chase,
As we fumble through this wild space.
For the map will twist and often bend,
Yet laughter remains a trusted friend.

In Search of the Hidden Answer

With magnifying glass in hand,
I sift through grains of distant sand.
Looking for wisdom, so profound,
But only find a funny clown.

He juggles questions, drops a few,
Shrugs off riddles, then bids adieu.
With every answer, just a tease,
Whispers of "Why not?" on the breeze.

I trace my steps through confused thoughts,
Life's riddles tangled in silly knots.
Yet every laugh brings clarity bright,
A secret answer hidden from sight.

So let's not rush, let's take a break,
For every riddle leads to a cake.
In search of wisdom, we may find,
Joy in the quest is intertwined.

The Secret Language of Hearts

We speak in giggles, winks, and sighs,
A language formed beneath the skies.
In every beat, a silly jest,
Hiding meanings that we know best.

A heart can giggle, a laugh can pulse,
In whispers soft, it may convulse.
With every thump, a joke is shared,
The punchline lands, and we've all bared.

So don't you fret about your place,
In the secret dance, find your grace.
For hearts have rhythms, bright and bold,
A melody of stories yet untold.

Let's sing our quirks, embrace the fun,
For in this language, we are one.
So share your heart with a silly cheer,
In the secret language, love is near.

Reflections in a Shattered Mirror

I looked at myself, what a sight!
With a grin that's not quite right.
The mirror cracked, a funhouse view,
Is that really me, or someone new?

Every shard tells a funny tale,
Of mistakes made and dreams that fail.
Yet in this chaos, I find delight,
In all the quirks that make life bright.

The Mysterious Path of Choices

Two roads diverged, which one to tread?
One's filled with snacks, the other dread.
I chose the snacks, what a surprise!
Turns out I'm just a donut in disguise.

Choices are like socks gone astray,
One blue, one pink, who needs the gray?
Each step I take, I laugh and grin,
For who knows where the fun will begin?

When Stars Align in Darkness

In the night sky, they twinkle bright,
Yet down here, I trip and bite.
Stars wink at me, say, 'Hey, what's up?'
I reply, 'Falling flat, so fill my cup.'

Cosmic humor in every glance,
While I stumble in this goofy dance.
They giggle softly, light my way,
Reminding me to laugh and stay.

A Symphony of Unanswered Queries

Questions float like bubbles in air,
Pop one too soon, and there's despair.
Why's the sky blue? What's for lunch?
Guess I'll ponder till I munch.

Notes of curiosity play a tune,
Under the watch of a silly moon.
In the orchestra of doubt, I sway,
Finding joy in questions every day.

Navigating the Ocean of Thoughts

Drifting on waves of what-ifs,
A seagull steals my sandwich, oh bliss!
Maps are lost in the foggy mind,
Where's the treasure I hope to find?

A compass points to 'maybe,' you see,
Navigating thought like a clown at sea.
Giggling as I swim 'round and 'round,
Sharks of doubt are lurking, unbound.

Sailing past clouds of 'could be,'
With a parrot who tells jokes, so free,
He squawks about life's silly gigs,
While I ponder the dance of figs.

But wait! Is that a starfish wearing a hat?
I blink my eyes. Can that be so fat?
Each twist and turn, a slapstick show,
As seaweed whispers secrets below.

The Mirage of Certainty

In the desert of thoughts, I chase a mirage,
Hoping for water, but it's just a barrage.
Lizards wear sunglasses, sipping on dreams,
I chuckle at shadows and giggly beams.

Sandstorms of questions swirl all around,
My confidence wobbles, like a clown on ground.
I fall in a cactus, but bounce back with flair,
Each poke tells a joke—ain't life a fair?

Palm trees chuckle at my plight,
As I twirl and tumble with all my might.
Palm wine fountains flow, or do they not?
I take a sip—this joke is quite hot!

But what if this mirage is all I need?
A riddle of sand where absurdities breed.
So I dance with the lizards, and sing out loud,
In the funhouse of thoughts, I'm feeling quite proud.

Secrets Beneath the Surface

Bubbles rise from thoughts, oh what a tease,
Fish in the pond giggle with ease.
What secrets do they keep inside?
Is it wisdom or a big fish guide?

I dive down deep, with my snorkel and fins,
Finding laughs where the silliness spins.
A clam snaps a joke, oh what a sound,
While seaweed dances, twirls all around!

Octopus winks with eight arms so sly,
Avoiding the questions—oh my, oh my!
While crabs do the cha-cha on the sandy floor,
I realize this riddle's a big overhead score.

So I swim with delight, amidst giggles and splashes,
Those silly fish thoughts create clever clashes.
Under the surface, it's a whimsical place,
Where secrets of nonsense finally embrace.

Traces of the Unexplained

In the attic of thoughts, dust bunnies dress,
Playing hide and seek, causing a mess.
What's that ticking? A clock or a bee?
It's a riddle that teases, just wait and see!

Footprints in the attic, but no one's there,
Maybe it's the ghost of a dancing bear?
Each creak of the floor tells a story, so bright,
Laughter echoes through the deepness of night.

In the cupboard, I find socks with holes,
Whispering secrets, those cheeky moles.
I put on a sock and it starts to run!
Chasing my thoughts—it's a wacky fun!

But who left the cookies? A mystery unfolds,
With chocolate crumbs left from stories told.
In the chaos of nonsense, one truth remains,
The funniest riddles are in our brains.

Questions Beneath the Stars

Why do we fumble with so many socks?
While time ticks away on the ancient clocks?
Do ducks really quack in a dignified way?
Or is it just nonsense they share every day?

Is cheese truly better when sprinkles are near?
Or do aliens coil when we laugh out of fear?
Do stars have a purpose or just like to twinkle?
Will we ever find out, or just sit and wrinkle?

Can a cat send a text while chasing its tail?
And does popcorn giggle when it starts to swell?
Why does the moon dance with clouds in the night?
As we try to solve all these riddles with fright?

What if a worm dreams of flying a kite?
And spaghetti blushes when served in the light?
So many questions that bounce through our heads,
We laugh while we ponder; it fills us with dread.

Journeying Through the Unknown

With sandals on feet, I wander so wide,
In search of great truths, with none as my guide.
Are jellybeans fruit if they're sweet to the taste?
Or do gummy bears cry, feeling wholly misplaced?

In a world of lost keys and socks full of holes,
Where I trip over logic while searching for goals.
Do we snort when we laugh or just chuckle out loud?
Or can laughter echo while standing in crowds?

Do pineapples wear hats to feel quite so chic?
Or is it just my mind, playing hide-and-seek?
In this journey of questions, the roads spin around,
As I dance with the thoughts that make giggles abound.

Perhaps wisdom's a fruit that's best shared with friends,
And even a joke has a path that it bends.
So I travel on boldly, with humor as fuel,
In a quest for fun answers; oh, ain't life a school?

Pondering the Unanswerable

What came first, the chicken or muffin surprise?
Do potatoes have dreams beneath their disguise?
Can a toaster feel lonely, just popping away?
Or does bread sing sweet songs to forget the day?

Do hedgehogs embrace when it rains in the park?
Or do squirrels organize secret meetings in dark?
Can rainbows taste better than pancakes at brunch?
Or is that just me when I munch and I crunch?

Do clouds ever gossip about us on the ground?
Or plot silly pranks with the winds all around?
Can laughter be bottled, and sold in a store?
Should I grab a few scoops and run for the door?

While pondering riddles that twist like a vine,
I find humor and joy in each jumbled line.
With questions that tickle and puns that excite,
I embrace all the chaos; it feels just so right.

The Map of Uncertainty

If I drew you a map with no roads and no signs,
Would you follow the paths traced in puddles and vines?
Do fish ever splurge on a fancy night out?
Or do they just shimmer and wander about?

Would socks still feel lonely if found in a pair?
Or do they enjoy sharing tales of despair?
If I ask a goldfish about life in a bowl,
Would it laugh at my questions or just roll and stroll?

In a maze made of marshmallows, sweet and unclear,
Do gummy bears bounce for the joy they hold dear?
Can clocks ever slumber without ticking their time?
Or do seconds just giggle, embracing the rhyme?

As uncertainty dances, we twirl and we spin,
With humor as armor, we laugh through the din.
In the puzzle of puzzling, so strange and absurd,
We map out our questions with joy undeterred.

Whispers in the Wind

A squirrel in a bowler hat,
Dancing with a feathered cat.
They whisper truths from tree to chair,
While we all just stand and stare.

The grass tickles at our toes,
As the garden gnome just dozes.
Wisdom flows like lemonade,
In the shade where jokes are made.

A button lost in all the fuss,
Promises of a cheeky bus.
To nowhere and then everywhere,
With giggles bursting in the air.

So laugh with me and take a chance,
For every frown can learn to dance.
We'll ride the winds of silly things,
Where joy can soar on wobbly wings.

Enigmas of the Heart

A heart-shaped balloon on a string,
Asks who'll be my silly king?
It floats and flutters here and there,
Dodging raindrops, happy flair.

The candy shop's an endless maze,
Where chocolates sing in sweet displays.
A lollipop that tells a joke,
Makes you laugh 'til you choke!

A dancing muffin, roll, and bun,
All gathering for fragile fun.
While whispers tickle in the dark,
As shadows tease with laughter's spark.

Oh, what a puzzle made of cheer,
Wrapped in ribbons far and near.
Unraveling bliss, a lovely art,
Uncovering enigmas of the heart.

Threads of Destiny

A spider weaves with wobbly grace,
Catching dreams in a knitted space.
Each thread a giggle, each knot a cheer,
What tangled tales will we all hear?

A sock with stripes, mismatched fun,
Says, "Together we have won!"
As the toaster sings a silly song,
With golden toast all day long.

Tickling toes in cotton clouds,
Wrapped in warmth, away from crowds.
A tapestry of laughter spun,
Each thread a joy, our hearts outrun.

Come join the dance of woven fate,
Where every twist seems just first-rate.
In the fabric of all we see,
Threads of humor stitch you and me.

The Labyrinth of Moments

In the maze of time, a duck does quack,
Waddling forward, never looking back.
Each twist and turn a comic play,
Where laughter lights the winding way.

A clock that spins, hands in a race,
Ticking backwards at a funny pace.
While moments giggle, slide, and glide,
Sneaking off with a wink and pride.

The paths are lined with candy treats,
And giggling maps with dancing beats.
Oh, how they twist, those silly paths,
Leading us to endless laughs.

So shall we run or shall we stroll?
Embrace the joy; it's good for the soul.
In the labyrinth of what we've planned,
It's the funny bits that truly stand.

The Riddle of Existence

Why do ducks wear little shoes?
To avoid those muddy blues!
But what's the point of a fish on a bike?
It might be fun, but who'd take a hike?

The cat meows with cosmic flair,
Pretending it's the emperor of air.
Meanwhile, the goldfish dreams of light,
In a bowl, plotting its grand flight.

Does the toaster know it's quite a star?
Or just get warm, not going too far?
A couch once said, "I'm tired of this,"
But who knew sofas could dream of bliss?

In the end, it's all a bluff,
We're guessing games, made of fluff.
With every laugh, we twirl and spin,
Unraveling wonders locked within.

A Symphony of Uncertainties

A chicken crossed to catch the bus,
While cows around just made a fuss.
Were they lost or just plain bored?
In this tune, we're all ignored.

A wink from fate, what could it mean?
Are jellybeans divine cuisine?
With every beat, the clock resounds,
Inquirers ask if truth surrounds.

The magic shoes dance on their own,
While gnomes debate the dangers of bone.
Is this a jest or fate's great play?
A riddle spun for every day.

As we hum this wild, absurd song,
We find the notes where we belong.
In laughter, we explore the space,
A quirky quest, a whimsical chase.

The Quest for Connection

Two socks were lost behind the dryer,
Now scheming, as the tales grow higher.
A quest for mates, oh what a show,
    Perhaps they're off to Idaho?

The toaster chats up the blender's song,
While the fridge hums along, not wrong.
In every hum, a bond we make,
Even when we're starting to quake.

If spoons could talk, what tales they'd weave,
Of midnight raids and cookie thieves.
Yet here we are, a motley crew,
In this kitchen, chaos ensues.

With every clink, we raise a cheer,
To friendships formed year after year.
In this funny mess of tangled fate,
We find connections that just can't wait.

The Spiral of Time

Time ticked on, a cheeky sprite,
Taking naps in the warm sunlight.
With every tick, it played its game,
A jester dressed in space and flame.

The past wore shoes that squeaked a lot,
While future danced in a courtyard plot.
Present just waved, with cheeky glee,
Still wondering what will come to be.

A spiral staircase leads to where?
Do we climb up or drop in despair?
With laughter echoing down each turn,
We discover all we wish to learn.

Time's tricky, like a cat's soft purr,
Changing shape, a fuzzy blur.
So here's to moments, round and round,
In the spiral, joy is found.

The Puzzle of Existence

Wake up each day, a new clue to find,
Why did I step on that gum, so unkind?
Puzzles unwrapped, I scratch my head,
Did I really just wear my socks in red?

With cereal choices, I twirl and I spin,
Each bowl a puzzle, where do I begin?
Milk or banana, which one should I pick?
The choices are endless, oh what a trick!

In chatter and banter, we laugh and we jest,
Each silly remark, life's quirky test.
A riddle of sorts, wrapped in delight,
Like shoes on my head, it feels just right!

So solve with a giggle, don't take it too hard,
Embrace the odd moments, it's not that bizarre.
For each twisty question, a chuckle awaits,
In this wacky adventure, let laughter dictate!

Echoes in the Labyrinth

Round every corner, a riddle does dance,
With jokes and with jests, life's curious chance.
Who left this sock? Oh, what a great find!
An echo of laughter that tickles the mind.

In a maze of confusion, we whirl and we twist,
With every misstep, we clench our fists.
A sandwich or laundry? What was my plan?
Lost in my thoughts, now I'm chasing a can!

A paradox wrapped in a peanut-butter spread,
Why is there ketchup around my bed?
The notes of the riddle are scattered and loud,
Like a cat that just knows it's better off proud!

With grins as my compass, I navigate through,
In this raucous confusion, I'm quite the debut.
So join in the laughter, don't let it be thin,
For echoes of joy make the best kind of din!

Whispers of a Mysterious Journey

Off on a quest, so quirky and bright,
With mischief and giggles, I stumble in fright.
Is that a sage, or just a wise frog?
Whispers of wisdom wrapped in a fog.

Through forests of shadows, I leap and I bound,
Each step filled with laughter, so joyously found.
Who knew that the squirrels could tell such a tale?
Or that ducks could sing, while the bunnies set sail?

Oh, what a journey, with riddles so grand,
I ponder the meaning, ice cream in hand.
With jokes on the breeze and giggles to share,
This mystical quest has become quite the fare!

So frolic and ball, in the curious maze,
With whispers of wonder that endlessly play.
For in every twist, there's humor to cling,
In the dance of existence, let joy be the swing!

The Tapestry of Questions

Threads of confusion woven so tight,
With chuckles and quips, we twinkle in light.
What's the best flavor, pickles or pie?
The tapestry shivers in the blink of an eye.

With each stitch a story, a colorful thread,
Did I really wear these shoes that are red?
Where's the cat hiding? Is he seeking my chair?
With questions a-plenty, it leads to despair!

Jokes are the colors that brighten the gloom,
Why does the broom still sweep, even in bloom?
The patchwork of puzzles unfolds with a laugh,
In this marvelous tapestry, we find our own path!

So gather the riddles and chuckles in sums,
In this wrinkled adventure, so whimsical, it hums.
For questions are threads in this joyous parade,
We weave a grand story, let fun never fade!

Illusions of Certainty

We chase the path so straight and clear,
A map that shifts with every year.
We think we know what's round the bend,
But turns out it's just a funny trend.

With plans like jelly on a wall,
We trip and laugh, we rise and fall.
The crystal ball's a market ploy,
It tells of woes, not of joy.

The ticking clock a cruel disguise,
It laughs at us with knowing eyes.
We stride with swagger, heads held high,
Then trip on shoelaces—oh my!

So smile wide with every twist,
For certainty's a fleeting mist.
In stumbles, giggles are the prize,
As we unlock the grand surprise.

The Unspoken Language

There's wisdom in a cat's sly grin,
While dogs bark loud, they never win.
A squirrel's scurry, all too quick,
Hides secrets in a nutty trick.

The birds converse in chirps and tweets,
While humans wear their dull, old cleats.
A wink, a nod, we'd like to think,
Means more than just an empty drink.

For every giggle wraps a tale,
Beneath the surface, we unveil.
A gopher's dance, a rabbit's hop,
Can tell a story, never stop.

So let's decode the laughter's sound,
And find the joy that knows no bound.
The world's a stage, a playful plot,
Where unspoken truths are never caught.

The Tapestry of Time

Time's a weaver with a thread,
Of laughter, tears, and things unsaid.
Each moment shines, then fades away,
A patchwork quilt of every day.

We stitch our dreams with clumsy hands,
Creating hopes like rubber bands.
A tangle here, a knot over there,
Yet find delight in every snare.

The past is but a silly prank,
Where we mistook the pause for rank.
Tick tock, tick tock, the clock will cling,
To moments that we thought were kings.

So weave your story, bright and bold,
In colors that can't be controlled.
For time's a joker, playing tricks,
And in the chaos, laughter picks.

Unraveled Dreams

We build our castles in the air,
Then trip on dreams without a care.
A blueprint sketched on napkin blue,
With all the plans that never grew.

Woken up by socks in pairs,
Reality checks—oh, how it flares!
A jumbled thought, a missed chance play,
Turns out, it's just a cloudy day.

But isn't it a funny sight,
To see a dream take off in flight?
With wings of felts and bits of yarn,
Our funny visions cause alarm.

So let's unwrap the jigs and jives,
The silly quirks that keep us alive.
In every failure, laughter beams,
For life's just full of unraveled dreams.

A Dance with the Unknown

A jester's hat on my head, I sway,
Twisting and turning in bizarre ballet.
With every step, a chuckle appears,
As questions pop up like mischievous cheers.

Who wrote the script? Do I even care?
I'm just here to dance, so why not dare?
The music's a riddle, a tune from the skies,
With notes that wink and wear papery ties.

So let's twirl around the answers we seek,
With laughter that echoes, a joyous peak.
For in stepping forward and making a leap,
We stumble upon secrets that twirl in a heap.

So waltz with me friend, to the rhythm of jest,
In this dance of the clueless, we're truly blessed.
With giggles and wiggles, together we'll glide,
Unlocking the riddles that everyone hides.

Beyond the Veil of Time

Tick-tock, the clock plays a silly tune,
It jumps and it skips, like a goofy cartoon.
Past meets the future in a dizzy twist,
Where everyone's puzzled, but who gets the gist?

A wise old turtle tells tales a bit slow,
While time runs in circles, like a shaky yo-yo.
Back to the future, or forward we flee,
Who knows where we go? Maybe just to the sea!

When seconds are snacks and minutes are dreams,
With laughter and jest in whimsical schemes.
So let's play with time, let's dance through the haze,
In this riddle of moments, let's leave 'em ablaze.

The past laughs with us, the future a tease,
As whooshing time tickles with playful unease.
So join in the fun, we're lost in the rhyme,
In a world where we giggle 'beyond the veil of time'.

The Riddle Wrapped in Silence

In a quiet room, whispers do prance,
Where secrets are hiding, awaiting their chance.
With silence so loud, it tickles the mind,
Unraveling puzzles that we never quite find.

A cat with a grin sits atop a great box,
Is it full of riddles or just some old socks?
With each silent pause, the heart plays a game,
While laughter erupts, as we try to frame.

So let's sip our tea, as we ponder and jest,
With riddles in silence, who knows what's best?
For laughter's the answer wrapped deep in the hush,
As we stumble in silence, a comedic rush.

So here's to the whispers and giggles that sprout,
In the quietest corners, there's humor throughout.
With silence as canvas, the jokes intertwine,
In a riddle wrapped snugly, we giggle and shine.

Journeys through the Mind's Maze

In a maze made of thoughts, I run and I trip,
With twists that confound, my sanity slips.
But oh, the delights in each crooked turn,
For laughter's the lantern that helps us to learn.

With signs pointing nowhere and paths made of dreams,
I follow my nose, 'cause it's better than schemes.
Each corner, a giggle, a jolt of surprise,
As the mind maps the riddles with comical skies.

A clue in the shadows, a grin from the wall,
Tickling my mind as I chuckle and sprawl.
Through jokes and confusions, I wander so free,
In this journey of humor, come laugh here with me!

So what's in the maze? Perhaps just some fun,
With riddles in laughter, we've already won!
Embrace all the quirks, let each twist amaze,
In this labyrinth of giggles, we're lost in the haze.

Paradoxes in Bloom

A cat walks free, yet stays confined,
Chasing its tail, it's so unkind.
A fish on land, yeah, that's a trick,
The world might just need a logic clock.

A rose that sings, oh what a surprise,
It blooms in silence, under blue skies.
Mice in tuxedos, they'd dance the night,
While cats just ponder, 'What is our plight?'

Colors that taste and sounds that can smell,
Where hilarity brews, there's always a spell.
The sun does a jig, the moon rolls its eyes,
In this jester's world of whimsical lies.

The Quest for Meaning

Why is the sky blue, they often inquire,
While fish fly high, like dreams that inspire.
A rooster sings at the break of noon,
Creating confusion, a comic cartoon.

Do ants hold conferences, set for the day?
Do they discuss crumbs and share in the play?
With plans for a picnic under the tree,
Oh, what a sight, we jest, can't you see?

The puzzles of puzzles, they muddle and mix,
As thoughts tumble down like clever little tricks.
But laughter rings true through every odd twist,
In this silly quest, let joy not be missed.

Fragments of Reality

A banana talks to a grumpy old shoe,
Says, 'Why the long face? Join the hullabaloo!'
While socks sneak away for a late-night spree,
The world's a big stage, just come out and see.

Clouds made of sugar bring rain made of tea,
A party for clouds, it's a sweet jubilee.
Kites play hide and seek with the breeze,
As trees tap dance, quite full of unease.

Mirrors that reflect but change what they show,
In this mild madness, we thrive and we grow.
Fragments of laughter will piece us complete,
In this quirky realm, oh, isn't it neat?

The Art of Becoming

A turtle that races, slow but so wise,
Says, 'Every step's art, it's all in disguise.'
While rabbits read books on how to be cool,
The art of becoming finds humor in school.

A cactus wears glasses, sharp yet so chic,
While shadows play chess, oh, it's quite the critique.
Jellybeans swim in the sea of delight,
Hoping to dance with the stars every night.

With hats made of dreams and shoes full of cheer,
We waltz through the questions that linger so near.
In the art of becoming, we giggle and cheer,
For every odd moment, we hold oh so dear.

Shadows of Tomorrow

In a world where cats can fly,
I ponder if I should try.
With shoes on my hands, I roam free,
What a strange fate that must be.

Chasing dreams in rainbow hues,
Pies in the sky, I can't refuse.
But why do my socks always mismatch?
Is it fate, or just a bad catch?

Lost in riddles from day to night,
Counting cows in pink delight.
What is the reason my phone won't ring?
Perhaps it's just my pet's next fling!

So here I stand, a jester's delight,
Wearing my glasses, all crooked in sight.
For every question I boldly ask,
Might just be part of the silly mask.

The Great Unraveling

Oh, the yarn of truth is tangled tight,
Like a cat who thinks it's a knight.
Unravel the mess, stitch by stitch,
Then trip on the tails, oh what a hitch!

Does the cake taste better with sprinkles, I ask,
While balancing spoons, it's quite the task.
For every answer that seems so grand,
There's a potato chip lost on the land.

Ah, but should I run from the big bad foe,
Or ask for a selfie, stealing the show?
Every mishap adds to the fun,
Especially when it all comes undone!

So let's twirl and spin, in a dizzy dance,
With socks on our heads, take a chance.
In this puzzle of nonsense, we smile and cheer,
For the unwrapped secrets are never clear!

A Mosaic of Choices

Life's a quilt of odd designs,
With jellybeans and tangled lines.
Should I pick purple or lime today?
Flip a coin and shout hooray!

What if the sun wore fuzzy hats?
Would we dance with the acrobatic rats?
"Choose wisely," they say with a wink,
But does it matter? I just can't think!

In the buffet of dreams, take a scoop,
Serve it up with a sprinkle of loop.
Adventure lies in choices we make,
Like picking a path on a pancake lake.

So grab a paintbrush, let's swirl about,
With colors of laughter, we'll never pout.
For every twist, and every turn,
Is a chance for joy; it's our time to learn!

The Dance of Uncertainty

Twisting and turning on a twirly chair,
What's the secret? Does anyone care?
With tangoing mice and a prancing goat,
The dance of the clueless, a funny quote!

Waltzing through choices like leaves in a breeze,
Should I sing loud or just do a sneeze?
Each moment a step, each laugh gives a twirl,
As we juggle with chaos in a dizzy whirl.

The fate of our steps is a wibbly wobbly thing,
A yo-yo in motion with no clear string.
Can we dance on the edge without fear or fright?
Or slip on a banana peel in the night?

But here's the trick, the secret we find,
With each little stumble, we'll never be blind.
For the dance of uncertainty, bold and bright,
Is a riotous journey, our hearts take flight!

The Infinite Quest

On a quest to find the truth,
I tripped over my own shoe.
Chasing answers in the dark,
I found a cat, and thought, 'how cute!'

Maps of logic twist and bend,
Each clue leads to a new trend.
With giggles echoing afar,
I'm lost, but hey, I found a star!

In the maze of thoughts I roam,
Searching for a slice of home.
An owl hoots, 'What's the fuss?'
I shrug and ride my magic bus!

Every question brings delight,
A hiccup in the name of insight.
As we ponder, laugh, and jest,
I think the riddle's just a test.

Landscapes of Wonder

In a field of dreams, I strolled,
With cows that whispered secrets bold.
One said, 'Why wear just one sock?'
I looked down and laughed in shock!

Mountains high, clouds floating low,
A wind that tickled, 'Where'd it go?'
Each valley holds a hidden joke,
The trees laugh too—who needs a cloak?

Rivers babble, sharing news,
While frogs debate their favorite muse.
Flowers giggle, petals wide,
Nature's humor, can't be denied!

In this world, so strange yet bright,
Every twist feels just so right.
With chuckles blending, less we doubt,
The riddle's fun; it's what it's about!

Secrets of the Universe

The stars conspire in twinkling light,
While planets have a brawl at night.
Black holes laugh, 'We're taking bets!'
It seems they've got no regrets!

Galaxies spin like a silly dance,
As comets wink—what a crazy chance!
Einstein's ghost is trading tips,
On how to dance with cosmic flips!

Each quasar sings a tune,
While asteroids hum a cartoon.
In the expanse where all things play,
Laughing physics rules the day!

With every wink from bright stars above,
The universe whispers: 'It's all about love!'
And as we ponder, just for fun,
It seems the riddle's never done!

The Language of the Heart

A heart beats with a rhythm strange,
In a world that's bound to change.
One day it gurgles, next it giggles,
Sending signals, mixing wiggles!

Love notes scribbled on a napkin,
Dancing dreams where fancies happen.
A heartbeat sighs, 'Do you feel this?'
Each thump whispers: 'Catch the bliss!'

In every smile, a tale unfolds,
As ice cream melts, and joy beholds.
With laughter bubbling, it's no debate,
The heart's a riddle, never late!

So let's embrace what we can't know,
In this dance of joy, we'll go with the flow.
A playful chase through every part,
Together we'll solve the riddles of the heart!

In Search of the Unfathomable

I searched for answers in my cereal bowl,
But found only soggy flakes with no soul.
The milk laughed softly, the spoon gave a grin,
That maybe the questions were where to begin.

I chased a butterfly, but it fled with a tease,
It danced on the breeze with such elegant ease.
I thought, 'What a riddle, this flighty delight,'
As I stumbled and tripped, to my sheer delight.

The sun wore a hat, with shades on its face,
While clouds played hide and seek, just keeping pace.
I asked the sun, 'Why do you shine so bright?'
It winked back at me and said, 'It's just a light!'

So here I stand, with a question or two,
In a world made of puzzles, life's surely askew.
But laughter is gold, with riddles to weave,
And I'll chase them forever—oh, what a reprieve!

The Mirror of Perception

I looked in the mirror, what a strange sight,
My hair stood on end, like it's taking flight.
The reflection just laughed, and turned to a pose,
Said, 'Is this really how the world goes?'

The cat in the corner, gave me a wink,
Said life's just a puzzle, or maybe a drink.
We pondered together on what's true and wrong,
As I tried to recall just where I belong.

I called up the moon, asked for some advice,
It replied, 'You're human, now isn't that nice?'
The stars giggled softly, their twinkle so bright,
Said, 'Chase the bizarre, and you'll win this fight!'

So here's to the mirrors, and the tricks that they play,
Each twist and turn adds laughter each day.
In a world full of wonders, it's clear to see,
With humor as a compass, we'll unravel the spree!

Unwritten Stories

The pages lay blank, just begging for ink,
A plot twist could happen with just one little blink.
The pencil rolled over, like it had a mind,
And giggled, 'Let's see what we can find!'

The chair creaked and moaned, like it had some sass,
Said, 'Write me a tale, oh please, make it last!'
But the cat just sat there, its tail held so high,
As if to announce that I'd soon be awry.

Each blank line a riddle, just waiting for fate,
A dragon, a knight, or a large dinner plate?
The plot thickened quickly, with a light-hearted flair,
As I spilled my coffee, saying, 'Who put this there?'

So I'll scribble and doodle, let the chaos ensue,
For every blank story has laughter in view.
With whimsy as my guide, on these pages I roam,
Creating my fables, I'll never feel alone!

The Riddle of Every Sunrise

Through sleepy eyes, the world starts to glow,
The sun yawns awake, saying, 'Here we go!'
The rooster crows proudly, what a silly sound,
As if it knows secrets that must be unbound.

The coffee pot bubbles, like a witch's brew,
While toast dances eagerly, frying in queue.
I ponder the morning—it's such a fine jest,
What riddle does breakfast have waiting as best?

Chasing the shadows, I stepped on a shoe,
That wasn't my own, but who knows what's true?
The world says, 'Good morning!' as I trip and I fall,
And I wonder if riddles are laughing at all.

With each rising dawn, new puzzles unfold,
The day whispers softly, 'Hey, be bold!'
So I'll greet the sun's riddle, armed with a grin,
For the joy of the journey is where we begin!

Fables of the Unseen

In the garden of questions, weeds grow wild,
The caterpillar wonders, is this all worthwhile?
With a wiggle and a squirm, it spins its grand tale,
But emerges a butterfly, with a wardrobe to hail!

A snail on a mission, slow and unchaste,
Sprints to the finish line, at a leisurely pace.
With confidence soaring, it shouts, "I can win!"
Turns out it was just in a race with the wind!

A rabbit once pondered, what makes humans tick?
He thought he might teach them, with his legendary tricks.

But they just stared blankly, as he hopped to and fro,
He sighed and decided, "I just won't show!"

In the maze of existence, with turns and some bends,
The secret to everything, it seems never ends.
But with giggles and grins, we'll scribble it down,
And crown every question, with the silliest crown!

The Cycle of Whys

Why does the chicken cross roads? What a fuss!
To prove to the possum, it's safe to discuss.
But the road had a plot twist, as two tires rolled by,
And both feasted on wings, while the chicken just sighed!

Why do we ponder the stars high above?
While the squirrels complain, there's no acorn to shove?
And on moonlit nights, they create quite the ruckus,
Challenging shadowy beings, oh what a circus!

Why do the flowers insist on their show?
Every spring they wake up, with grandeur to blow.
But when summer rolls in, they just wilt and they pout,
And mumble of winter, while the bees flit about!

Why do we chase what can hardly be grasped?
In a world full of slip-ups, might as well laugh!
For every great 'why,' there's a punchline in tow,
And the journey of questions is the best kind of show!

The Beauty of Complexity

A puzzle unravels, with pieces that tease,
Like socks in the dryer, they're hard to appease.
With colors that clash and a picture unclear,
The fun in the chaos is what draws us near!

The cat in the hat thinks he's clever and sly,
Building towers of dishes, oh my, oh my!
But when gravity giggles, the stack makes a fall,
And the cat learns quickly—there's beauty in all!

The ants in their army march strict, line by line,
But stop when a kid pedels over, oh divine!
As they scatter in laughter, confusion takes flight,
Yet together they gather, to march back with might!

Life's quirks and its tangles are what make it sweet,
Like whipped cream on pickles, a most curious treat.
So let's toast to the twists, in every grand step,
For complexity's charm makes us giggle and prep!

Echoes of Forgotten Paths

In the forest of choices, where lost socks reside,
Echoes of giggles, where few dare to stride.
A squirrel points left, while the rabbit goes right,
And a dance of confusion ensues in the night!

A wise owl once hooted, "What's the best way?"
The mice just nodded, then dashed off to play.
Though trails twist and tangle, and seem misaligned,
Each echo leads somewhere, you'll surely find!

The trails are all tangled, like spaghetti on plates,
But that makes each venture an adventure of fates.
With each turn we take, don't forget to just smile,
For each bumbling error adds spice to the mile!

So wander, dear friend, through the echoes of time,
Meet the hedgehogs and turtles, all taking their climb.
Though paths may be blurry, look closely and see,
The fun in the echoes is where you'll be free!

Fragments of the Unseen

In a sea of socks, I find a shoe,
A mismatched puzzle in shades of blue.
The cat just laughs, as it slips away,
Why do we chase what won't even stay?

With coffee spills and toast that burns,
It's clear, the universe has its turns.
A dance of chaos, a twirl of fate,
Who knew breakfast could be so late?

The clock ticks loud, but I'm in a daze,
Trying to remember if I paid for today.
With silly hats and mismatched socks,
Is it really me, or am I in a box?

A riddle unfolds, a laugh, a twist,
Each moment's a joke that you can't resist.
So here's to the chaos, the funny side,
In this strange journey, let's take a ride!

Unfolding Chronicles of Being

I tripped on dreams while wearing shoes,
Stumbling in questions, what to choose?
The map is blank, I've lost the key,
But the chocolate cake is calling me!

A circus of thoughts, they juggle wide,
With a wink and a nod, they take the ride.
Every wrong turn is just a change,
Like finding new ways to rearrange.

With twisty paths and bumps to break,
Finding the humor in every mistake.
The universe chuckles at plans so grand,
As I chase my tail, is it all just a stand?

So laugh it off, don't take it to heart,
In this grand play, we all take part.
For what's the fun in a straight line?
Let's dance with the quirks, and make it divine!

The Enigma of Each Breath

What's the deal with yesterday's toast?
It didn't ask to be a breakfast ghost.
Each breath is a riddle, a giggle, a sigh,
Why do we worry when birds just fly?

In gardens of jest, with daisies spun,
The secrets of giggles are just began.
Wit's a fine friend, and irony too,
Making mischief in shades of blue.

When clocks melt down, just like in dreams,
Time's but a trickster, or so it seems.
With every heartbeat, a silly prank,
Who will be the one to thank?

So take a step with laughter's grace,
And join the chase in this zany race.
For answers are funny, like the ducks that waddle,
With every breath, let's solve this riddle!

Shadows in the Dawn

In morning's glow, the shadows play,
A squirrel drops acorns; who's in the fray?
Tickling the dawn with giggles so bright,
While the toaster's humming, it's toast-errific night!

What's it all about? The sun winks back,
With pancake flips on this merry track.
Each shadow dances to its own beat,
Who knew breakfast could taste so sweet?

As coffee brews in its faithful pot,
The day's still young, what a funny thought!
Each step through mirth, each laugh a song,
Bringing light to where we all belong.

In sunrise whispers, the riddles tease,
And laughter continues, just like the breeze.
With shadows and giggles as friends by our side,
Let's take on the riddle with hearts open wide!

www.ingramcontent.com/pod-product-compliance
Lightning Source LLC
Chambersburg PA
CBHW070750220426
43209CB00083B/386